CHECK PLEASE

A SHORT COMEDY BY
Jonathan Rand

The Rules in Brief

1) Do NOT perform this Play without obtaining prior permission from Playscripts, and without paying the required royalty.

2) Do NOT photocopy, scan, or otherwise duplicate any part of this book.

3) Do NOT alter the text of the Play, change a character's gender, delete any dialogue, cut any music, or alter any objectionable language, unless explicitly authorized by Playscripts.

4) DO provide the required credit to the author(s) and the required attribution to Playscripts in all programs and promotional literature associated with any performance of this Play.

For more details on these and other rules, see the opposite page.

Copyright Basics

This Play is protected by United States and international copyright law. These laws ensure that authors are rewarded for creating new and vital dramatic work, and protect them against theft and abuse of their work.

A play is a piece of property, fully owned by the author, just like a house or car. You must obtain permission to use this property, and must pay a royalty fee for the privilege—whether or not you charge an admission fee. Playscripts collects these required payments on behalf of the author.

Anyone who violates an author's copyright is liable as a copyright infringer under United States and international law. Playscripts and the author are entitled to institute legal action for any such infringement, which can subject the infringer to actual damages, statutory damages, and attorneys' fees. A court may impose statutory damages of up to $150,000 for willful copyright infringements. U.S. copyright law also provides for possible criminal sanctions. Visit the website of the U.S. Copyright Office (www.copyright.gov) for more information.

THE BOTTOM LINE: If you break copyright law, you are robbing a playwright and opening yourself to expensive legal action. Follow the rules, and when in doubt, ask us.

Playscripts, Inc.
450 Seventh Ave, Suite 809
New York, NY 10123

toll-free phone: 1-866-NEW-PLAY
email: info@playscripts.com
website: www.playscripts.com

Dedicated to Christy

For your free consulting services,
Breathtaking vocal stylings,
And your friendship

Cast of Characters

GIRL
GUY

LOUIS
MELANIE
KEN
MARY
MARK
PEARL
TOD
SOPHIE
BRANDON
LINDA
MANNY
MIMI

Setting

A restaurant. Two dinner tables.

Time

Now.

Production Note

This play was originally written with the intention of having the same two actors play the roles of Girl and Guy, and having 12 different actors play the rest of the roles. Another fun option would be to cast the play using four total actors, with all 12 dates split between two quick-change artists. The other option (which I least prefer) would be to cast every scene with a different pair of actors. While this would be a great opportunity to get more people involved in the production, it ends up weakening the character development of Girl and Guy, as well as the play's conclusion.

Check Please, West Columbus High School, Cerro Gordo, North Carolina (2003).

CHECK PLEASE
by Jonathan Rand

Scene 1

LOUIS. Hi.

GIRL. Hi there.

LOUIS. It's great to meet you.

GIRL. You, too.

LOUIS. So how long have you lived in the city?

GIRL. Almost a year. Feels longer, though.

LOUIS. Three years for me. It's a great city.

GIRL. Definitely. What do you like most about it?

LOUIS. What do you like most about living here?

(*Pause, as* GIRL *is only slightly noticeably confused.*)

GIRL. Well...I love walking my dog in the park. Especially on a pretty day.

LOUIS. Oh yeah? I'm a little different, I guess. I'm more the kinda guy who likes walking my dog in the park on a pretty day.

(*He chuckles.*)

GIRL. Same here.

LOUIS. Oh and also — and this may just be me — but I have this thing for walking my dog in the park on a pretty day.

GIRL. No, I like that, too. I just said so.

LOUIS. So do you like watching TV?

GIRL. No.

LOUIS. Me, too! I love it!

(*Pause.*)

GIRL. Are you listening to me at all?

LOUIS. Sometimes I like to curl up with a bag of popcorn and get my Leno on. You like Leno?

GIRL. You really aren't listening.

LOUIS. Me, too! Jay Leno just cracks — me — up.

GIRL. This is ridiculous…

(Throughout the monologue below, GIRL gradually tries out different tactics to see how self-centered and non-reactive LOUIS truly is. She tries saying things to him like "excuse me" and "hello"; she tries whistling at him; she might try touching his nose with her index finger or a spoon for a few seconds; she could try walking over to him and temporarily turning his chair in the opposite direction. No matter what she does, LOUIS just keeps on trucking, as if she wasn't there.)

LOUIS. I mean, his comedy is a gift from the gods. You know what I'm talking about? I just get blown away every time I see his show, or one of his movies. Did you see *Ice Age 2?* You haven't? Stop what you're doing and rent it *now.* I'm telling you, Leno is the funniest guy on television, no doubt about it. He reminds me of me, actually. We have the same sense of humor. My roommate, Bill? He says I'm the funniest person he's ever met. I mean, he's entitled to his opinion, right? Anyway, sure I'm funny, but I've got my personality flaws. For example, sometimes I'm *too* funny. People don't realize it when I'm being serious!! Do you believe that?! But hey, enough about me. I'm talking up a storm here! Tell me about you.

GIRL. Or I could just leave now, since you're a self-centered tool.

(A pause; we assume he is going to break.)

LOUIS. I'm a Capricorn myself.

(Blackout.)

Scene 2

GUY. Hi.

MELANIE. Hi.

GUY. It's so great to finally meet you.

MELANIE. Same here!

GUY. So where are you fr—

MELANIE. Wait, before you— Sorry. *(Meekly:)* This is so rude, but the Bears game is on right now? You don't mind if I check the score…

GUY. Oh, not at all. Totally.

MELANIE. *(As she pulls out her cell phone to check her web-browser:)* Thanks. I know this is such an awful thing to do on a first date, but it's late in the fourth quarter in a playoff game.

GUY. No worries.

MELANIE. Is it all right with you if I wear this earpiece? I promise it won't be distracting.

GUY. What's the score?

MELANIE. Packers by seven.

GUY. Uh-oh.

MELANIE. Nah, it's no big deal. It's just a game, right? So c'mon— enough about football. Let's hear about "Mister Mystery." Harriet's told me tons about you.

GUY. Man... The pressure's on now.

> *(They laugh together, genuinely. MELANIE's laugh then fades directly into her next line, which is suddenly serious.)*

MELANIE. I'm just gonna check one more time.

> *(She digs into her purse.)*

GUY. *(Smiling:)* No worries.

MELANIE. Is it all right with you if I put on this little earpiece thingy? It won't be distracting, I promise.

GUY. Sure.

MELANIE. *(As she puts the earpiece in her ear:)* I'm making the worst first impression, aren't I...

GUY. Not at all.

MELANIE. It's just because it's the playoffs. I'm usually normal.

GUY. It's really no—

MELANIE. Come on!!

GUY. What?

MELANIE. Oh, nothing—the line only gives Forte this huge running lane, but he fumbles the handoff. Sure, Pace recovered, but come on—this is the playoffs. You don't just cough up the ball like that. Now you're staring at third and long, and the whole season is riding on one play.

GUY. I hope ev—

MELANIE. WHAT?!

GUY. What?

MELANIE. PASS THE BALL!!

GUY. What's wrong?

MELANIE. It's third and long— Who runs it on third and long? Did Cutler suddenly FORGET that he has an ARM?!

> (GUY *looks around subtly at the other patrons.*)

Oh my God. I'm being loud, aren't I.

GUY. (*Trying hard to be convincing:*) No…

MELANIE. Oh, I am. I'm so sorry. Look, how about this: I'll make it up to you. After dinner I'll buy you dessert at this tiny little bistro on 11th that nobody knows about. I think you'll just—PASS THE BALL!! Jesus, people! It's FOURTH DOWN! Pass the FRIGGING BALL!

GUY. Listen—we could go to a bar with a TV or something.

MELANIE. Oh please, no. I wouldn't do you that to you. The game's pretty much over anyway. (*She takes a deep breath, and is now very calm.*) Okay. I'm done. I got a little carried away there, didn't I? Let's order.

> (*They peruse for a moment, as if nothing has happened.*)

GUY. (*Indicating the menu:*) Oh. Harriet said we should definitely try the—

> (MELANIE *suddenly lets out a bloodcurdling shriek and rips the menu in half.*)

GUY. Or we could order something else.

MELANIE. (*Downtrodden:*) They lost…

GUY. Oh. I'm sorry.

MELANIE. (*Starting to tear up:*) They lost. The season's over..

GUY. Well—

> (MELANIE *breaks down, bawling.* GUY *thinks for a moment, then takes out a handkerchief and offers it to* MELANIE. *She uses it to blow her nose.*)

GUY. I'm so sorry. Is there anything I can do?

MELANIE. (*Still weepy:*) The Bears suck…

GUY. Aww, no. They don't suck.

MELANIE. They do… They suck.

GUY. They're probably just having a bad season—

(MELANIE *grabs his collar, pulls him extremely close, and speaks in a horrifying, monstrous, deep voice.*)

MELANIE. THE BEARS SUCK.

GUY. *(Weakly:)* The Bears suck.

(*Blackout.*)

Scene 3

GIRL. Hi.

KEN. Hello.

(*He kisses her hand, lingering there a second too long.*)

GIRL. It's great to meet you.

KEN. The pleasure…is all mine.

GIRL. So…where are you from? I can't place the accent.

KEN. I was raised in the mountains of Guam…and was born…on the shore of New Jersey.

(*Beat.*)

GIRL. Do you want to order some appetizers?

KEN. Anything…which will ensure happiness for your beautiful lips.

(*He looks at menu, unaware of her subtle look of disbelief. She finally looks down at her menu.*)

GIRL. Ooh! The shrimp cocktail looks good.

KEN. Shrimp… A creature of the ocean. The ocean…which is not nearly as lovely as the ocean of your eyes.

GIRL. Listen, can I ask you sort of a…blunt question?

KEN. Anything which your heart desires will be—

GIRL. Yeah yeah. Are you going to be like this for the rest of dinner?

KEN. Whatever do you mean?

GIRL. You know, all creepy and nauseating?

(Pause.)

KEN. Yes.

    (Blackout.)

Scene 4

GUY. Hi.

MARY. Hi.

GUY. It's so great to finally meet you.

MARY. Same here! Listen: I was wondering if you were free next Friday.

GUY. Uh, I think so. Why?

MARY. Well, if dinner goes well tonight, I wanted to go ahead and schedule a second date.

GUY. Oh. Okay, sure.

MARY. See, 'cause here's the thing: My parents are having a house-warming party at their new place on August 2nd, and if you and I hit it off tonight and end up getting serious, that party would be the perfect opportunity for you to meet them, so I'd like to squeeze in six dates beforehand, because if we don't, my parents might be skeptical of our relationship, which, after you pop the question, could make everyone uncomfortable during the ceremony, which could then carry over during our three-week honey¬moon in Cozumel, and most important than anything else, it could really take a toll on little Madison.

    (Pause.)

GUY. Wow…

MARY. What? What is it? You don't like the name Madison? We could change it. My second, third, and fourth choices are Fiona, Riley, and Apple.

GUY. No, all of those are…great names…

MARY. Something's on your mind. You know can always tell your little bunny rabbit *anything*.

GUY. The problem is: you seem to have our whole relationship figured out—and we just met thirty seconds ago. I mean, you've got everything pinned down but the wedding dress.

MARY. Does that make you uncomfortable?

> *(Beat.)*

(As she withdraws several boxes:) Because if it does, we can pick it out now.

> *(Blackout.)*

Scene 5

> *(Lights up to MARK dressed in nothing but a burlap sack. He's looking at the menu, as if nothing is out of the ordinary. GIRL is looking at him, expressionless. After several moments, he folds the menu, his dinner decision made. He looks up. Pause.)*

MARK. *(Innocent:)* What?

> *(Blackout.)*

Scene 6

GUY. Hi.

PEARL. Hi.

GUY. It's so nice to meet you.

PEARL. Same here. Julia's told me a lot about you.

GUY. She's a great girl.

> *(The moment GUY begins speaking the above line, PEARL quickly and slickly steals a fork. GUY thinks he saw wrong. PEARL continues on as if nothing has happened.)*

PEARL. Yeah. So much fun to be around. We've been friends for something like...six years, I think?

GUY. *(As PEARL quickly steals the rest of the utensils:)* Where'd you meet? In school?

PEARL. Yeah. We played soccer. Both second-stringers, keeping the bench nice and warm for everyone else.

> *(They laugh together. During their laugh, PEARL swipes her napkin.)*

Seriously, Julia is one of my favorites. And she's got great taste, so when she told me about you, I was definitely on board.

(The moment GUY begins speaking the next line, PEARL swiftly and deftly removes the flower from the vase, pours the contents of her glass into the vase, pockets the glass, and replaces the flower in the vase.)

GUY. That's very — sweet...

PEARL. No, really — I've been looking forward to this for a while.

GUY. *(As PEARL takes the flower:)* I'm flattered.

PEARL. So... You hungry? I'm about ready.

> *(PEARL picks up her menu; GUY does likewise. The moment GUY begins speaking, PEARL slides the menu into her jacket.)*

GUY. I'm pretty hungry, too — you know, I can see that you're stealing. You don't have to play it off like you're not.

PEARL. What? What are you talking about?

GUY. *(As PEARL steals a plate:)* I'm sitting right here — See? There. You just stole a plate.

PEARL. Wow...that's a cruel accusation...

GUY. *(As PEARL steals sugar holder:)* Accusation?! I'm watching you steal those sugar packets right now? How can you honestly believe I don't notice.

PEARL. *(Starting to leave:)* Look, I don't know what your problem is with me as a person, but this is really insulting. I'd better go.

GUY. Wait. Listen: if you'll stop stealing things, I won't get on your case. Okay?

> *(Pause.)*

PEARL. Okay...

GUY. Yeah?

PEARL. Yeah...

GUY. Great. So where are you from — ?

> *(She whips the tablecloth off the table and starts stuffing it down her pants.)*
>
> *(Blackout.)*

Scene 7

(GIRL is sitting across from TOD, a little boy — regardless of the age of the actor portraying this role, it should be immediately and abundantly clear that TOD is far too young for GIRL. A long pause.)

GIRL. This may sound insensitive, but…how old are you?

TOD. What's yer favorite animal?

GIRL. No, I'm serious. I really want to know your age.

TOD. I like elephants.

GIRL. I think there's been a misunderstanding. See, when your profile said you were still in school, I assumed you meant college —

(She is suddenly interrupted by TOD's elephant impression. Beat.)

GIRL. That's very lifelike.

TOD. Do you have a scar? I have a scar! Do you want to see it?

GIRL. No, that's all right.

(Before she can finish her thought, TOD throws his leg up on the table, rolls up his pant leg, and shows the scar on his knee.)

TOD. I got it from kickball. Do you see it?

GIRL. Honestly, how old are you?

TOD. *(A quick display on his fingers:)* This many. Will you be my girlfriend?

GIRL. Your girlfriend.

TOD. 'Cause Katie Johnson always brings boring lunch to school and Courtney Shuler smells like horses.

GIRL. You've got a lot of girlfriends.

TOD. Yeah will you be my girlfriend?

GIRL. *(Sarcastically giving in:)* Sure… But only if you pay for dinner.

TOD. Okay.

(He produces a huge piggy bank and begins emptying change. Blackout.)

Scene 8

(SOPHIE *enters the restaurant. She is a very old woman, edging toward the table in a walker.* GUY *just stares. Blackout.*)

Scene 9

(BRANDON *and* GIRL *are in mid-laugh.*)

BRANDON. I didn't even —

GIRL. —I know, I know —

BRANDON. —I mean, seriously!

GIRL. —I know, right?

(*They settle down from the laughter.*)

BRANDON. So listen — all joking aside…this is fun! I'm really having a good time.

GIRL. Me, too! This has been great.

BRANDON. Hasn't it?

GIRL. Ugh! There's a fly in my water.

BRANDON. Gross. Here, take mine. (*To offstage:*) Waiter? Can we get another water?

GIRL. You are so sweet.

BRANDON. Ah, c'mon.

GIRL. No really.

BRANDON. Anyone would do that.

GIRL. Actually, you'd be surprised. With the luck I've been having on dates…

BRANDON. Really? But you're so fun. And beautiful.

GIRL. Oh please.

BRANDON. No. I mean it.

GIRL. You are just too good to be true.

BRANDON. C'mon, Robin.

(*Pause.*)

GIRL. What?

BRANDON. What?

GIRL. Who?

BRANDON. What?

GIRL. Who's Robin?

BRANDON. What do you mean?

GIRL. You just called me Robin. Who's Robin?

>   (BRANDON *fidgets.*)

GIRL. Is it your girlfriend?

BRANDON. No.

GIRL. Who is she?

BRANDON. He.

GIRL. He?

BRANDON. He.

GIRL. You're gay?

BRANDON. No! Well, yes. But Robin's my agent. I'm an actor.

GIRL. You're gay.

BRANDON. Yeah.

>   (*Pause.*)

GIRL. And why am I on a date with you?

BRANDON. Okay… I'm sorry I didn't tell you this sooner, but it would've totally backfired if I did. Here's the deal: I'll be playing Stanley in a local production of Streetcar, and since I'm a method-actor, I won't be able to get the part down until I method-act straight.

GIRL. Method-act.

BRANDON. Yes. I can't be Stanley Kowalski until I truly experience what it feels like to woo a woman.

>   (*Pause.*)

GIRL. So let me see if I can follow: you had me get dressed up for dinner, drive all the way downtown, and get my hopes destroyed after thinking I'd finally met a halfway decent guy—all so you could get a better feel for being straight?

>   (*Beat.*)

BRANDON. You don't mind, do you?

(Pause. She takes her glass of water and douses his face. Pause.)

BRANDON. Oh my god. That was perfect! The ultimate heterosexual dating moment! I've got it! I'm in! I'm straight! STELLAAA-AAAAAAAA —

(She grabs the other glass of water and douses his face again.)

(Blackout.)

(Note: The character of Brandon should NOT be played as flamboyantly gay — the audience should only be made aware of that fact when he explains it during the date. The actor should play the part completely straight throughout.)

Scene 10

LINDA. Hi.

GUY. Hi.

LINDA. I've been looking forward to this for a while.

GUY. Me, too. Sorry about all the rescheduling.

LINDA. Pssh, whatever, it's cool. Oh, shoot. Hold on. I forgot to —

(She starts rummaging through her purse, and after a couple of seconds, dumps it on the table and starts looking through the items.)

GUY. What's up? What's wrong?

LINDA. Oh, it's this silly thing. I've got this pill I need to take or else I get all weird. *(Back to her purse:)* I know I brought them. They've gotta be — You know, whatever. I'll be fine.

GUY. You sure? We could go to a pharmacy or something.

LINDA. Nah it's no big deal. It's just a precautionary drug, you know? It won't kill me if I don't take it for one night. I just may be a little out of whack. You probably won't even be able to tell. Whatever. So — anyway.

GUY. *(Smiling:)* Anyway.

LINDA. It's nice to finally meet you.

GUY. The feeling's mutual.

LINDA. *(Suddenly sarcastic, morose, in a monotone voice:)* Oh yes. It's so *awesome* to finally put a name with a face.

GUY. Heh. Yeah. Seriously.

LINDA. *(Giggly/bubbly:)* You're funny; you're cute.

    (Gruff:) He's not cute. You just haven't been out in a while.

    (Snobby:) That is NOT — TRUE. He is GOOD — LOOKING.

    (Jittery:) Shhhhhhhh… You're embarrassing yourself…

    (Aggressive:) Quit freaking out.

    (Easily offended:) What? Why are you jumping all over me?

    (Little girl:) She started it!

    (Motherly:) Girls, don't fight. What would your father say.

    (Fatherly:) Oh, let 'em fight.

GUY. Are you okay?

LINDA. *(Aggressive, to* GUY:*)* You stay out of this!

    (Reasonable:) Hey, leave him alone. You just met him.

    (Gruff:) Oh, he can take care of himself

    (Monkey:) Ooh ooh, ah! ah! ah!

    (Snobby:) All right, who brought the monkey?

    (Assertive:) Not me.

    (Little girl:) Not me.

    (Gruff:) Not me.

    (Pushover:) I did. I'm so sorry.

    (Aggressive:) A monkey? Come on!

    (Motherly:) You'd better behave yourself young lady, or you're grounded.

    (Fatherly:) Get off her case, woman!

    (Monkey:) Ooh ooh AHH AAHHH!

    (GUY *notices a bottle and shows it to* LINDA.*)*

GUY. Hey, are these the pills?

LINDA. *(Cheery:)* There they are!

    (Gruff:) Yeah, took long enough.

    (LINDA *swallows the pill.)*

GUY. Is everything all right?

LINDA. *(Mostly back to normal, but woozy:)* Okay. Okay. It's starting to kick in.

GUY. Great.

LINDA. In a couple of seconds, I'll settle into a single personality. But don't worry — nine times out ten it's one of the normal ones.

GUY. But with my luck —

> (LINDA *suddenly lets out a monkey shriek, grabs some bread from the table, sniffs it voraciously, stuffs it in her mouth, and lumbers offstage.)*
>
> *(Pause.)*

GUY. She was nice.

> *(Blackout.)*
>
> *(Note: Linda's personality switches should be fast. Each personality should be a different level — her voice and demeanor should be changing dramatically throughout.)*

Scene 11

GIRL. Hello.

MANNY. Hi.

GIRL. It's nice to meet you.

MANNY. Same.

GIRL. Let's order. I'm starved.

MANNY. Me, too.

GIRL. Wow, this menu's huge!

MANNY. I can never decide when the menu's so big. I can be picky.

GIRL. Ooh! I'm definitely getting the pork chops. What about you?

MANNY. I don't know. Nothing really leaps out.

GIRL. Really? Why don't you tryyyy — the pot roast.

MANNY. Nooo — too moist.

GIRL. Okay. How about…the shrimp scampi.

MANNY. Too moist.

GIRL. Oh.

MANNY. I actually have a tiny bit of hygrophobia.

GIRL. Hygrophobia?

MANNY. It's the fear of dampness or moisture.

GIRL. Oh, okay. How about the eggplant parmesan?

MANNY. Porphyrophobia.

GIRL. What's that?

MANNY. Fear of purple.

GIRL. You could get the cheese plate.

MANNY. Coprastasophobia.

GIRL. Fear of…?

MANNY. Constipation.

GIRL. What about the sushi?

MANNY. Japanophobia. *(Beat.)* It's the fear of —

GIRL. No, I got it. What about this Hawaiian fish? Let's see if I can pronounce it right: Humuhumunukunukuapua'a'.

MANNY. That actually sounds delicious.

GIRL. Great!

MANNY. But I suffer from a rare case of hippopotomonstrosesquippedaliophobia.

GIRL. Which is?

MANNY. Fear of long words.

GIRL. Okay! How about this: peanut butter and jelly.

MANNY. Sorry.

GIRL. What could possibly be wrong with peanut butter and jelly?

MANNY. I recently developed arachibutyrophobia.

GIRL. Fear of sandwiches?

MANNY. Fear of peanut butter sticking to the roof of my mouth.

GIRL. So what can you eat?

MANNY. NNot much. I do have sitiophobia.

GIRL. Fear of…?

MANNY. Food.

GIRL. Right. So if you have all of these dietary issues, why did you ask me to *dinner?*

MANNY. Good question.

GIRL. Look, how about we just skip this and go to a hockey game or something.

MANNY. Oooh, can't. Pacifist.

GIRL. Mini-golf.

MANNY. Asthma.

GIRL. See a musical.

MANNY. Dependson the musical; I have ailurophobia.

GIRL. Fear of…?

MANNY. Cats.

> *(Beat.)*

GIRL. Well, what would you like to do?

MANNY. Well, I have one or two ideas.

GIRL. Great.

MANNY. But I have decidophobia.

GIRL. Okay, I'll decide for you. How about we call it a night?

MANNY. I can't.

GIRL. Why not?

MANNY. Anuptaphobia?

GIRL. *(Sarcastic:)* What's that? Fear of staying single for the rest of your life?

MANNY. Actually, yes.

GIRL. Oh.

MANNY. On the other hand, it's probably best we end the date now, on account of my deipnophobia..

GIRL. Fear of…?

MANNY. Dinner conversations.

> *(Beat.)*

GIRL. Okay, well in that case, have a good night.

> *(She extends her hand for a friendly handshake.)*

MANNY. You, too! One second.

> *(He takes out a pair of rubber gloves and starts to put them on.)*
>
> *(Blackout.)*

Scene 12

> *(GUY is sitting across the table from a fully outfitted mime, MIMI, who, throughout the scene, is extremely over-the-top and exuberant, as stereotypical mimes are. The scene begins with MIMI "leaning" on "something." Mimed actions in this scene will be indicated with brackets. A few moments pass, as we get a feel for the absurdity of the scenario.)*

GUY. So what do you do for a living…?

> *(Beat.)*

MIMI. [Pulling something heavy with a rope.]

GUY. You pull rope. *(Pause.)* Look… I respect your profession. I think it's noble what you do… The world needs more people who… climb invisible ladders. But I really don't see how it's appropriate to bring your work to a date.

MIMI. [Battling against harsh winds.]

GUY. Oh yeah, quite a storm in here.

> *(GUY opens his menu and reads. MIMI mimes picking up an imaginary menu, and peruses it page after page. GUY looks up and watches MIMI do her thing.)*

GUY. Okay, I'm gonna go…use the restroom.

> *(GUY gets up, takes his jacket from the back of the chair.)*

MIMI. [You're leaving? Driving away? Far? Bye bye?]

GUY. No, I'm not leaving. I'm taking my jacket with me because…it might get cold in the men's room.

MIMI. [Cold like me in this wild blizzard?]

GUY. Yeah, cold like that.

> *(GUY starts to leave. MIMI follows close behind, maybe as an airplane pilot, or a bus driver.)*

GUY. No, you stay here. You —

MIMI. [Let me feed some chickens. Awww, those chicks are adorable. I love petting these lovely animals.]

GUY. I don't know what that is… Look I have to…

> *(An idea dawns on GUY has an idea. The following is an extremely loud and animated sequence of events — very frantic for MIMI; sarcastically frantic for GUY.)*

GUY. Oh, okay… *(Looking up:)* Oh my God! A BOX!

MIMI. [Where? Where?]

GUY. A huge, glass box, falling from the sky!!

MIMI. [Oh no! Oh no! I can't see it! What in heavens name will I do! Help me!]

GUY. Noooooooo!

> *(GUY follows "the box" with his finger as it plops directly on the frantic MIMI, who is now very much "trapped" inside the box. Blackout.)*

Scene 13

> *(Lights up to MARK in his burlap sack. He is reading the menu. Long pause.)*

GIRL. I give up.

MARK. If you've got a problem with me, why don't you just say it to my face?

GIRL. Okay. You're wearing a burlap sack.

> *(Beat.)*

MARK. It's Versace..

> *(Beat.)*

GIRL. *(As she stands to leave:)* I need to go powder my nose.

> *(GIRL exits toward GUY's table. The lights on GIRL's table remain up as lights come up on GUY's table. MIMI is still in her box, but she doesn't distract from the main action. GIRL and GUY bump into each other.)*

GIRL. Oh, sorry.

GUY. No, no. My fault.

(A short moment of instant chemistry. Then GUY shakes it off, as does GIRL.)

GUY. Well, goodnight.

GIRL. Goodnight.

(They start to go their separate ways.)

GUY. Hold on a second. *(Pause.)* This may seem random, but... do you like football?

GIRL. A little. *(Beat.)* Do you own any burlap?

GUY. No.

(Beat.)

GIRL. Should we go get some ice cream?

GUY. Yes.

(They exit together. A few moments pass. MIMI finally finds a "key" in her "pocket," unlocks the "door" to the "box" and exits. She moves to MARK, "spits" in her hand exuberantly, and extends it to him for a handshake. MARK looks up and notices what is going on in front of him.)

MARK. *(Deadpan:)* Check please.

End of Play